CONTENTS

ACKNOWLEDGMENTS

The publisher would like to thank the companies and organizations listed below for the use of their recipes and photographs in this publication.

American Lamb Council

The Hidden Valley® Food Products Company

Hillshire Farm®

Hormel Foods, Carapelli USA,
LLC and Melting Pot Foods Inc.

Jennie-O Turkey Store®

The Kingsford® Products Co.

National Honey Board

National Turkey Federation

Norseland, Inc. / Lucini Italia Co.

Reckitt Benckiser Inc.

Wisconsin Milk Marketing Board

Wisconsin Edam and Beer Spread

Makes 4 cups

1 ball (2 pounds) Wisconsin Edam Cheese*
¾ cup butter, cubed and softened
2 tablespoons snipped fresh chives
2 teaspoons Dijon mustard
½ cup amber or dark beer, at room
    temperature
  Pumpernickel or cocktail rye bread slices

Wisconsin Gouda can be substituted for Edam. Since Gouda is not available in ball form, this spread can be served in your favorite serving bowl.

Cut one fifth from top of cheese to create flat surface. With butter curler or melon baller, remove cheese from center of ball leaving ½-inch-thick shell. Shred enough of cheese removed from ball and top to measure 4 cups. Reserve remaining cheese for another use.

In large bowl, place shredded cheese, butter, chives and mustard; mix with spoon until blended. Stir in beer until blended. Spoon spread into hollowed cheese ball; reserve remaining spread for refills. Chill until serving time. Serve as spread with cocktail bread.

*Favorite recipe from **Wisconsin Milk Marketing Board***

APPETIZERS

4

Nachos con Queso y Cerveza

Makes 4 servings

4 ounces tortilla chips
Nonstick cooking spray
¾ cup chopped red onion
2 jalapeño peppers,* seeded and chopped
3 cloves garlic, finely chopped
2 teaspoons chili powder
½ teaspoon ground cumin
1 boneless skinless chicken breast (about
  8 ounces), cooked and chopped
1 can (14½ ounces) diced tomatoes, drained
⅓ cup pilsner lager
1 cup (4 ounces) shredded Monterey Jack
  cheese
2 tablespoons chopped black olives

*Jalapeño peppers can sting and irritate the skin; wear rubber gloves when handling peppers and do not touch eyes. Wash hands after handling.

1. Preheat oven to 350°F. Place chips in 13×9-inch baking pan.

2. Spray large nonstick skillet with cooking spray. Heat over medium heat. Add onion, peppers, garlic, chili powder and cumin. Cook and stir 5 minutes. Stir in chicken, tomatoes and pilsner. Simmer until liquid is absorbed.

3. Spoon tomato-chicken mixture over chips; top with cheese and olives. Bake 5 minutes or until cheese melts. Serve immediately.

APPETIZERS

5

Beer Cheese Dip

Makes about 3 cups

2 cups shredded Cheddar cheese
2 packages (8 ounces each) cream cheese, softened
1 packet (1 ounce) HIDDEN VALLEY® The Original Ranch® Salad Dressing & Seasoning Mix
½ to ¾ cup beer
  Chopped green onion
  Additional Cheddar cheese

In medium bowl, combine Cheddar cheese, cream cheese and salad dressing & seasoning mix. Gradually stir in beer until mixture is to desired consistency. Garnish with green onion and additional Cheddar cheese. Serve with pretzels or assorted fresh vegetables, if desired.

Polenta Triangles with Amber Ale

Makes 8 servings

½ cup yellow corn grits
½ cup amber ale
1 cup chicken broth
2 cloves garlic, minced
1 cup (4 ounces) crumbled feta cheese
1 jar (2 ounces) diced pimientos

1. Combine grits and ale in small bowl; mix well and set aside. Pour chicken broth into large heavy saucepan; bring to a boil. Add garlic and moistened grits; mix well and return to a boil. Reduce heat to low; cover and cook 20 minutes. Remove from heat; add feta cheese. Stir until cheese is melted. Add pimientos; mix well.

2. Spray 8-inch square pan with nonstick cooking spray. Spoon grits mixture into prepared pan. Press grits evenly into pan with wet fingertips. Cover and refrigerate until cold.

3. Spray grid with nonstick cooking spray. Prepare grill for direct cooking. Turn polenta out onto cutting board; cut into 2-inch squares. Cut each square diagonally into 2 triangles.

4. Place polenta triangles on grid. Grill over medium-high heat 1 minute or until bottoms are lightly browned. Turn triangles over; grill until browned and crisp. Serve warm or at room temperature.

APPETIZERS

Zesty Cheese Fondue

Makes 16 servings (4 cups)

1 package (1.8 ounces) white sauce mix
2 cups beer
1 clove garlic, minced
1 package (16 ounces) pasteurized process cheese spread, cubed
3 tablespoons *Frank's® RedHot® Original Cayenne Pepper Sauce*
1 loaf French or Italian bread, cubed
Apple slices

1. Prepare white sauce mix in large saucepan according to package directions except substitute beer for milk and add garlic. Stir in cheese; cook, stirring constantly, until cheese melts and sauce is smooth. Stir in **Frank's RedHot** Sauce.

2. Transfer sauce to fondue pot or heated chafing dish. Serve warm with bread cubes and apple slices.

Prep Time: 15 minutes
Cook Time: 10 minutes

Bock Bean Bites

Makes about 30 appetizers

1 cup chunky salsa
1 cup refried beans
¼ cup bock beer or dark lager
2 tablespoons canned minced chilies
2 tablespoons chopped fresh cilantro
½ teaspoon ground cumin
3 large (10-inch) flour tortillas
1 cup (4 ounces) shredded Mexican cheese
  blend

1. Pour salsa into strainer; let drain at least 20 minutes.

2. Meanwhile, combine refried beans, beer, chilies, cilantro and cumin in small bowl; mix well. Preheat oven to 400°F. Spray baking sheet lightly with nonstick cooking spray; set aside.

3. Cut each tortilla into 2½-inch circles with round cookie cutter (9 to 10 circles per tortilla). Spread each tortilla circle with refried bean mixture, leaving ¼ inch around edge. Top each with heaping teaspoon drained salsa; sprinkle with about 1 teaspoon cheese.

4. Place tortillas on prepared baking sheet. Bake about 7 minutes or until golden brown.

Guadalajara Beef

Makes 4 servings

1 bottle (12 ounces) dark beer
¼ cup soy sauce
3 cloves garlic, minced
1 teaspoon ground cumin
1 teaspoon ground chili powder
½ teaspoon ground red pepper
1 beef flank steak (about 1 pound)
6 medium red, yellow or green bell peppers,
  seeded and cut lengthwise into quarters
8 (6- to 8-inch) flour tortillas
Sour cream
Salsa

1. Combine beer, soy sauce, garlic, cumin, chili powder and red pepper in large resealable plastic food storage bag; knead bag to combine. Add beef and seal. Refrigerate up to 24 hours, turning occasionally.

2. Preheat grill. Remove beef from marinade; discard remaining marinade. Place steak on grid over medium heat. Grill, uncovered, 17 to 21 minutes for medium rare to medium or until desired doneness, turning once. Grill bell peppers 7 to 10 minutes or until tender, turning once.

3. Cut steak across the grain into thin slices and serve with bell peppers, tortillas, sour cream and salsa.

BEEF

Stout Beef Bundles

Makes 8 servings

1 pound ground beef
½ cup sliced green onions
1 clove garlic, minced
⅔ cup chopped water chestnuts
½ cup chopped red bell pepper
¼ cup stout, such as Guinness
2 tablespoons hoisin sauce
1 tablespoon soy sauce
2 tablespoons chopped fresh cilantro
1 or 2 heads leaf lettuce, separated into
    leaves (discard outer leaves)

1. Brown ground beef in medium skillet; drain fat. Add onions and garlic. Cook until tender. Stir in water chestnuts, bell pepper, stout, hoisin and soy sauce. Cook, stirring occasionally, until bell pepper is crisp-tender and most of liquid has evaporated. Remove from heat.

2. Stir in cilantro. Spoon ground beef mixture onto lettuce leaves; sprinkle with additional hoisin sauce, if desired. Wrap lettuce leaf around ground beef mixture to make bundles.

Tip: *Slice additional green onions into long strips and use to tie leaves in place around bundles.*

BEEF

Best Beef Brisket Sandwich Ever

Makes 10 to 12 servings

1 beef brisket (about 3 pounds)
2 cups apple cider, divided
1 head garlic, cloves separated, slightly crushed and peeled
2 tablespoons whole peppercorns
⅓ cup chopped fresh thyme *or* 2 tablespoons dried thyme leaves
1 tablespoon mustard seed
1 tablespoon Cajun seasoning
1 teaspoon ground cumin
1 teaspoon celery seed
1 teaspoon ground allspice
2 to 4 whole cloves
1 bottle (12 ounces) dark beer
10 to 12 sourdough sandwich rolls, halved

SLOW COOKER DIRECTIONS

1. Place brisket, ½ cup cider, garlic, peppercorns, thyme, mustard seed, Cajun seasoning, cumin, celery seed, allspice and cloves in large resealable plastic food storage bag; seal. Refrigerate; marinate overnight.

2. Place brisket and marinade in slow cooker. Add remaining 1½ cups apple cider and beer.

3. Cover; cook on LOW 10 hours or until brisket is tender. Strain sauce; pour over meat. Slice brisket and place on sandwich rolls.

BEEF

Brewed Beef Enchiladas

Makes 2 servings

2 sheets (20×12 inches) heavy-duty foil,
    sprayed with nonstick cooking spray
6 ounces 90% lean ground beef
¼ cup sliced green onions
1 teaspoon fresh minced or bottled garlic
1 cup (4 ounces) shredded Cheddar cheese
    or Mexican cheese blend, divided
¾ cup chopped tomato, divided
½ cup frozen corn, thawed
⅓ cup cold cooked white or brown rice
¼ cup salsa or picante sauce
6 (6- to 7-inch) corn tortillas
½ cup Mexican lager
½ cup enchilada sauce
½ cup sliced romaine lettuce

1. Preheat oven to 375°F. Cook beef in medium nonstick skillet over medium heat until no longer pink; drain. Add green onions and garlic; cook and stir 2 minutes. Combine meat mixture, ¾ cup cheese, ½ cup tomato, corn, rice and salsa; mix well. Spoon mixture down center of tortillas. Roll up; place seam side down on foil sheet, three to a sheet. Mix lager and enchilada sauce; spread over tortillas.

2. Double fold sides and ends of foil to seal packets, leaving space for heat circulation. Place on baking sheet. Bake 15 minutes or until hot. Remove from oven; open packets. Sprinkle with remaining ¼ cup cheese; seal packet. Bake 10 minutes more. Serve with lettuce and remaining ¼ cup tomato.

BEEF

13

Hickory Beef Kabobs

Makes 4 servings

1 pound boneless beef top sirloin or tenderloin steaks, cut into 1¼-inch pieces
2 ears fresh corn, shucked, cleaned and cut crosswise into 1-inch pieces
1 green bell pepper, cut into 1-inch squares
1 small red onion, cut into ½-inch wedges
½ cup beer
½ cup chili sauce
1 teaspoon dry mustard
2 cloves garlic, minced
3 cups hot cooked white rice
¼ cup chopped fresh parsley

1. Place beef, corn, bell pepper and onion in large resealable food storage bag. Combine beer, chili sauce, mustard and garlic in small bowl; pour into bag. Seal bag tightly, turning to coat. Marinate in refrigerator 1 to 8 hours, turning occasionally.

2. Prepare grill for direct cooking. Cover 1½ cups hickory chips with cold water; soak 20 minutes.

3. Drain beef and vegetables, reserving marinade; thread onto 4 (12-inch) metal skewers. Brush with reserved marinade. Drain hickory chips; sprinkle over coals. Place kabobs on grid. Grill kabobs, uncovered, over medium heat 5 minutes. Brush with reserved marinade; turn and brush again. Discard remaining marinade. Continue to grill 5 to 7 minutes for medium or until desired doneness. Combine rice and chopped parsley; serve kabobs over rice mixture.

BEEF

Brisket of Beef

Makes 10 to 12 servings

1 beef brisket (about 5 pounds), trimmed
4 cloves garlic, minced
½ teaspoon black pepper
2 large onions, cut into ¼-inch slices and
   separated into rings
1 bottle (12 ounces) chili sauce
¾ cup beer
2 tablespoons Worcestershire sauce
1 tablespoon packed brown sugar

1. Preheat oven to 350°F. Place brisket, fat side up, in shallow roasting pan. Spread garlic evenly over brisket; sprinkle with pepper. Arrange onions over brisket. Combine chili sauce, beer, Worcestershire sauce and sugar; pour over brisket and onions. Cover with heavy-duty foil or roasting pan lid.

2. Roast 2 hours. Turn brisket over; stir onions into sauce and spoon over brisket. Cover; roast 1 to 2 hours more or until fork-tender. Transfer brisket to cutting board. Tent with foil; let stand 10 minutes.*

3. Stir juices in roasting pan. Spoon off and discard fat from juices. Carve brisket across grain into thin slices. Spoon juices over brisket.

At this point, brisket may be covered and refrigerated up to 1 day before serving. To reheat brisket, cut diagonally into thin slices. Place brisket slices and juice in large skillet. Cover; cook over medium-low heat until heated through.

BEEF

Scandinavian Burgers

Makes 4 servings

1 pound 90% lean ground beef
¾ cup shredded zucchini
⅓ cup shredded carrots
2 tablespoons finely minced onion
1 tablespoon chopped fresh dill *or*
    1 teaspoon dried dill weed
½ teaspoon salt
   Dash black pepper
1 egg, beaten
¼ cup beer
4 whole wheat or rye rolls (optional)

1. Prepare grill for direct cooking.

2. Combine ground beef, zucchini, carrots, onion, dill, salt and pepper in medium bowl; mix lightly. Stir in egg and beer; mix lightly until blended. Shape into four patties.

3. Grill over medium heat, covered, 8 to 10 minutes (or, uncovered, 13 to 15 minutes) to medium (160°F), turning once. Serve on whole wheat buns or rye rolls, if desired.

BEEF

Smoky Barbecued Beef Sandwiches

Makes 6 servings

2 large onions, cut into thin slices
1 beef brisket (about 3 pounds), trimmed
½ teaspoon salt
¾ cup beer (not dark)
½ cup packed light brown sugar
½ cup ketchup
1 tablespoon plus 1½ teaspoons
    Worcestershire sauce
1 tablespoon plus 1½ teaspoons soy sauce
2 cloves garlic, minced
2 chipotle peppers in adobo sauce, minced
1 teaspoon adobo sauce from can
6 kaiser or hoagie rolls, split and toasted

1. Preheat oven to 325°F. Separate onion into rings. Place in bottom of large roasting pan. Place brisket, fat side up, over onions; sprinkle with salt. Combine remaining ingredients except rolls in small bowl; pour over brisket. Cover with foil. Roast 3 to 3½ hours until brisket is fork-tender.

2. Transfer brisket to cutting board, leaving sauce in pan; tent brisket with clean foil. Let stand 10 minutes.

3. Skim fat from pan juices; discard. Transfer juices to large saucepan. Cook over medium heat until thickened, stirring frequently. Trim fat from brisket; carve brisket across grain into thin slices. Return slices to sauce; cook until heated through. Serve brisket and sauce on rolls.

BEEF

Spicy Italian Beef

Makes 8 to 10 servings

1 boneless beef chuck roast (3 to 4 pounds)
1 jar (12 ounces) pepperoncini
1 can (14½ ounces) beef broth
1 can (12 ounces) beer
1 package (1 ounce) Italian salad dressing
   mix
1 loaf French bread, cut into thick slices
10 slices provolone cheese (optional)

SLOW COOKER DIRECTIONS

1. Trim fat from roast. Cut roast, if necessary, to fit in slow cooker, leaving meat in as many large pieces as possible.

2. Drain pepperoncini; pull off stem ends and discard. Add pepperoncini, broth, beer and salad dressing mix to slow cooker; *do not stir.* Cover; cook on LOW 8 to 10 hours.

3. Remove meat from slow cooker; shred with 2 forks. Return shredded meat to slow cooker; mix well.

4. Serve on French bread, topped with cheese, if desired. Add additional sauce and pepperoncini, if desired.

Note: *Pepperoncini are thin, 2- to 3-inch-long mild pickled peppers. Look for them in the Italian foods or pickled foods section of the grocery store.*

BEEF

Patrick's Irish Lamb Soup

Makes 8 servings

1 tablespoon olive oil
1 medium onion, coarsely chopped
1½ pounds fresh lean American lamb boneless
    shoulder, cut into ¾-inch cubes
1 bottle (12 ounces) beer
1 teaspoon seasoned pepper
2 cans (14½ ounces each) beef broth
1 package (about 1 ounce) brown gravy mix
3 cups cubed red potatoes
2 cups thinly sliced carrots
2 cups shredded green cabbage
⅓ cup chopped fresh parsley (optional)

In 3-quart saucepan with cover, heat oil. Add onion and sauté until brown, stirring occasionally. Add lamb and sauté, stirring until browned. Stir in beer and pepper. Cover and simmer 30 minutes.

Mix in broth and gravy mix. Add potatoes and carrots; cover and simmer 15 to 20 minutes or until vegetables are tender. Stir in cabbage and cook just until cabbage turns bright green. Garnish with chopped parsley, if desired.

Favorite recipe from **American Lamb Council**

LAMB

19

Western Lamb Riblets

Makes 6 servings

5 pounds lamb riblets, cut into serving-size pieces
¾ cup bottled chili sauce
½ cup beer
½ cup honey
¼ cup Worcestershire sauce
¼ cup finely chopped onion
1 clove garlic, minced
½ teaspoon crushed red pepper flakes

Trim excess fat from riblets. In saucepan, combine chili sauce, beer, honey, Worcestershire sauce, onion, garlic and pepper flakes. Bring mixture to a boil. Reduce heat; simmer, covered, 10 minutes. Remove from heat; cool.

Place riblets in resealable plastic food storage bag. Pour cooled marinade over riblets in bag. Close bag securely and refrigerate about 2 hours, turning bag occasionally to distribute marinade evenly.

Drain riblets; reserve marinade. Arrange medium-hot KINGSFORD® Briquets around drip pan. Place riblets on grid over drip pan. Cover grill; cook 45 minutes, turning riblets and brushing with marinade twice. Bring remaining marinade to a boil; serve with riblets.

LAMB

Braised Lamb Shanks with Jarlsberg

Makes 4 servings

LAMB

- 4 lamb shanks (about 1 pound each)
- 2 tablespoons Lucini Premium Select extra virgin olive oil
- 1 chopped onion
- 2 minced garlic cloves
- 1½ cups beer
- 1½ cupsbeef broth

COATING

- 1 cup (4 ounces) shredded JARLSBERG cheese
- 1 cup flavored bread crumbs
- 1 teaspoon crumbled dried rosemary
  Freshly ground black pepper, to taste
- ⅔ cup cooking liquid from lamb shanks

In large, heavy skillet, brown 4 shanks in olive oil. Add onion and garlic. Cook until golden. Add beer and beef broth. Cover; simmer 1½ hours or until fork tender. Remove to platter. To reduce cooking liquid, cook over high heat, 5 minutes. Strain, defat and set aside.

Preheat oven to 325°F. Combine cheese with bread crumbs, rosemary, pepper and ⅔ cup cooking liquid. Divide mixture into 4 parts. Pat firmly on meaty tops and sides of lamb shanks to "blanket." Place shanks on rack in baking pan. Bake 15 to 20 minutes or until coating is firm and nearly crisp. Serve with white beans, salad and crusty bread. Serve remaining pan juices in gravy boat.

LAMB

Brats 'n' Beer

Makes 4 servings

1 can or bottle (12 ounces) beer (not dark)
4 bratwurst (about 1 pound)
1 sweet or Spanish onion, thinly sliced and
    separated into rings
1 tablespoon olive oil
¼ teaspoon salt
¼ teaspoon black pepper
4 hot dog buns

1. Prepare coals for direct grilling.

2. Pour beer into heavy medium saucepan with ovenproof handle. (If not ovenproof, wrap heavy-duty foil around handle.) Place saucepan on grill. Pierce bratwurst with knife; add to beer. Simmer, uncovered, over medium coals 15 minutes, turning once.

3. Place onion rings on heavy-duty foil. Drizzle with oil; sprinkle with salt and pepper. Fold sides of foil over rings to enclose. Place packets on grill. Grill, uncovered, 10 to 15 minutes or until onion rings are tender.

4. Transfer bratwurst to grill. Remove saucepan from grill; discard beer. Grill bratwurst 10 minutes or until browned and cooked through, turning once. Place bratwurst in buns. Top with onions. Garnish as desired.

PORK

Kielbasa & Kraut Heroes

Makes 8 servings

- 1 tablespoon vegetable oil
- 2 large red onions, cut in half lengthwise and thinly sliced
- 2 pounds kielbasa, thickly sliced
- 2 pounds sauerkraut, rinsed and well drained
- 1 can (12 ounces) beer
- ½ cup *French's®* Bold n' Spicy Brown Mustard
- 1 tablespoon caraway seeds
- 8 hot dog or hero-style buns

1. Heat oil in large nonstick skillet over medium heat. Add onions; cook 5 minutes or just until tender, stirring often. Remove from skillet.

2. Add kielbasa to skillet; cook and stir 5 minutes or until lightly browned. Drain well. Stir in sauerkraut, beer, mustard and caraway seeds. Cook over low heat 10 minutes or until most of liquid is absorbed, stirring occasionally. Serve in buns.

Tip: *This recipe may be prepared ahead. To reheat, place mixture in 12×9-inch disposable foil pan; cover. Place on grid; cook over medium heat 15 minutes, stirring occasionally.*

Prep Time: 20 minutes
Cook Time: 20 minutes

PORK

23

Ale'd Pork and Sauerkraut

Makes 6 to 8 servings

1 jar (32 ounces) sauerkraut, undrained
1½ tablespoons sugar
1 bottle (12 ounces) amber ale or dark beer
3½ pounds boneless pork shoulder or pork butt
½ teaspoon salt
¼ teaspoon garlic powder
¼ teaspoon black pepper
   Paprika

SLOW COOKER DIRECTIONS

1. Place sauerkraut into slow cooker. Sprinkle sugar evenly over sauerkraut; pour beer over all. Place pork, fat side up, on top of sauerkraut mixture; sprinkle evenly with remaining ingredients.

2. Cover; cook on HIGH 6 hours.

3. Remove pork to serving platter. Remove sauerkraut with slotted spoon; arrange around pork. Spoon about ½ to ¾ cup cooking liquid over sauerkraut, if desired.

PORK

Bacon and Cheese Rarebit

Makes 6 servings

12 slices bacon
1 small loaf (8 ounces) egg bread or challah,
    cut into 6 (1-inch-thick) slices
1½ tablespoons butter or margarine
½ cup beer (not dark)
2 teaspoons Worcestershire sauce
2 teaspoons Dijon mustard
⅛ teaspoon ground red pepper
2 cups (8 ounces) shredded American cheese
1½ cups (6 ounces) shredded sharp Cheddar
    cheese
12 large slices ripe tomato

1. Cook bacon in large skillet over medium-high heat about 7 minutes or until crisp. Remove bacon to paper towels. Toast bread slices until golden brown. Cover and keep warm.

2. Preheat broiler. Meanwhile, melt butter in double boiler set over simmering water. Stir in beer, Worcestershire, mustard and red pepper; heat through. Add cheeses, stirring constantly about 1 minute or until melted. Remove from heat; cover and keep warm.

3. Arrange toast on foil-lined 15×10-inch jelly-roll pan. Top each serving with 2 tomato slices and 2 slices bacon. Spoon about ¼ cup cheese sauce evenly over each serving. Broil 4 to 5 inches from heat 2 to 3 minutes or until cheese begins to brown.

PORK

Cajun Chicken Nuggets & Grilled Fruit

Makes 4 servings

½ cup beer
¼ cup *French's*® Bold n' Spicy Brown Mustard
2 tablespoons oil
1 pound boneless skinless chicken breasts,
    cut into 1½-inch pieces
¾ cup plain dry bread crumbs
1 tablespoon plus 1 teaspoon prepared
    Cajun seasoning blend
1 pineapple, peeled, cored and cut into
    ½-inch-thick rings
2 peaches, cut into 1-inch-thick wedges

1. Combine beer, mustard and oil in large bowl. Add chicken pieces; toss to coat evenly. Cover; marinate in refrigerator 20 minutes.

2. Preheat oven to 350°F. Coat baking sheet with nonstick cooking spray. Combine bread crumbs and Cajun seasoning in pie plate. Remove chicken from marinade; roll in bread crumb mixture to coat. Discard any remaining marinade. Place chicken on prepared baking sheet. Bake 20 minutes or until light golden brown and no longer pink in center, turning once. Remove to serving plate.

3. Coat fruit with nonstick cooking spray. Place fruit on oiled grid. Grill 5 to 8 minutes over medium heat until just tender. Serve with chicken nuggets and Peachy Mustard Glaze (recipe follows).

Peachy Mustard Glaze

¾ cup peach preserves
¼ cup *French's*® Classic Yellow® Mustard
2 tablespoons orange juice

Microwave preserves in small bowl on HIGH (100%) 2 minutes or until melted, stirring once. Stir in mustard and orange juice.   *Makes 1 cup*

Chicken Vera Cruz

Makes 4 to 6 servings

1 chicken (3 pounds), cut up
1 jar (12 ounces) salsa
1⅓ cups *French's*® French Fried Onions, divided
½ cup Spanish stuffed olives, sliced
½ cup beer
2 tablespoons lemon juice
2 tablespoons chopped fresh parsley
¼ teaspoon ground black pepper
Cooked white rice (optional)

Preheat oven to 350°F. Place chicken in 2-quart shallow dish. Bake, uncovered, 40 minutes. Drain.

Combine salsa, ⅔ cup French Fried Onions, olives, beer, lemon juice, parsley and pepper in medium saucepan. Bring to a boil. Reduce heat to low. Cook and stir 5 minutes or until slightly thickened. Pour sauce over chicken. Bake 15 minutes or until chicken is no longer pink near bone. Sprinkle with remaining ⅔ cup onions. Bake 5 minutes or until onions are golden. Serve with rice, if desired.

POULTRY

Bratwurst & Grilled-Onion Hoagies

Makes 5 servings

1 tablespoon butter or margarine
1 large onion, thinly sliced, separated into rings
½ teaspoon paprika
¼ teaspoon salt
¼ teaspoon freshly ground black pepper
1 package JENNIE-O TURKEY STORE® Lean Turkey Bratwurst
½ cup beer
2 teaspoons olive or vegetable oil
5 hoagie or submarine sandwich rolls, split, lightly toasted
Spicy brown mustard (optional)

Melt butter in large skillet over medium-high heat. Add onion rings; cook 3 minutes or until wilted, stirring occasionally. Sprinkle with paprika, salt and pepper. Reduce heat to medium-low; cook 15 to 20 minutes or until golden brown and tender, stirring occasionally. Meanwhile, combine bratwurst and beer in large saucepan. Cover and simmer 10 minutes. Pour off and discard liquid. Add oil to pan; brown bratwurst on all sides, about 6 minutes. Serve in rolls topped with onions, and, if desired, mustard.

POULTRY

Irish Stout Chicken

Makes 4 servings

2 tablespoons vegetable oil
1 medium onion, chopped
2 large cloves garlic, minced
1 whole chicken (3 to 4 pounds), cut into
    serving pieces
5 carrots, peeled and chopped
2 parsnips, peeled and chopped
1 teaspoon dried thyme leaves
¾ teaspoon salt
½ teaspoon black pepper
¾ cup stout, such as Guinness
½ pound fresh button mushrooms
¾ cup frozen peas

1. Heat oil in large skillet over medium heat until hot. Add onion and garlic; cook and stir 3 minutes or until tender. Remove vegetables with slotted spoon to small bowl.

2. Arrange chicken in single layer in skillet. Cook over medium-high heat 5 minutes per side or until lightly browned. Add onion and garlic mixture, carrots, parsnips, thyme, salt and pepper to skillet. Pour stout over chicken and vegetables. Bring to a boil over high heat. Reduce heat to low. Cover and simmer 35 minutes.

3. Add mushrooms and peas to skillet. Cover; cook 10 minutes.

4. Uncover skillet; increase heat to medium. Cook 10 minutes or until sauce is slightly reduced and chicken is no longer pink in center.

Turkey Kielbasa with Cabbage, Sweet Potatoes and Apples

Makes 6 servings

1 bottle (12 ounces) dark beer or ale
2 tablespoons Dijon mustard
½ teaspoon caraway seeds
6 cups coarsely shredded cabbage
1 pound fully cooked turkey kielbasa or
    smoked turkey sausage, cut into 2-inch
    pieces
1 Granny Smith apple, cut in ¼-inch wedges
1 can (16 ounces) sweet potatoes, cut into
    1½-inch cubes

1. Combine beer, mustard and caraway seeds in large deep skillet. Bring to a boil over high heat. Add cabbage. Reduce heat to medium-low. Cover; cook 5 to 8 minutes or until cabbage is crisp-tender.

2. Add kielbasa, apple and sweet potatoes. Increase heat to high. Bring mixture to a boil. Reduce heat to medium-low. Cover; cook 3 to 5 minutes or until apple is crisp-tender.

Favorite recipe from **National Turkey Federation**

Rick's
Good-As-Gold Chili

Makes 4½ cups

Nonstick cooking spray
¼ cup minced onion
2 teaspoons minced garlic
2 boneless skinless chicken breasts (about 16 ounces), cooked and cut into ¼-inch cubes
1 can (15 ounces) tomato sauce
¾ cup beer
½ cup chicken broth
2 tablespoons chili powder
2 teaspoons ground cumin
1 teaspoon dried oregano leaves
1 teaspoon soy sauce
1 teaspoon Worcestershire sauce
¾ teaspoon salt
½ teaspoon paprika
½ teaspoon ground red pepper
¼ teaspoon turmeric
⅛ teaspoon rubbed sage
⅛ teaspoon dried thyme leaves
⅛ teaspoon dry mustard

1. Heat large skillet with cooking spray over medium-high heat. Add onion and garlic; cook and stir 5 minutes or until golden.

2. Add remaining ingredients; stir well. Bring chili to a boil; reduce heat and simmer 20 minutes, stirring occasionally, until chili thickens slightly. Garnish, if desired.

POULTRY

31

Grilled Chicken with Chili Beer Baste

Makes 8 servings

2 tablespoons vegetable oil
1 small onion, chopped
1 clove garlic, minced
½ cup ketchup
2 tablespoons brown sugar
2 teaspoons chili powder
2 chipotle peppers in adobo sauce, minced
1 teaspoon dry mustard
½ teaspoon *each* salt and black pepper
3 bottles (12 ounces each) pilsner beer, divided
½ cup tomato juice
¼ cup Worcestershire sauce
1 tablespoon lemon juice
2 whole chickens (3½ pounds each), cut up

1. Heat oil in medium saucepan over medium heat. Cook and stir onion and garlic until tender. Combine next 7 ingredients in medium bowl. Add 1 bottle of beer, tomato juice, Worcestershire sauce and lemon juice; whisk. Add to onion mixture. Cook sauce until reduced to 2 cups. Cool; refrigerate overnight.

2. Divide chicken between 2 large resealable food storage bags. Pour remaining 2 bottles beer over chicken; seal bags. Refrigerate overnight.

3. Prepare grill for direct grilling; oil grid. Remove chickens from marinade. Grill over medium-hot coals, 20 minutes or until chicken reaches 175°F. Brush with baste during last 10 minutes of cooking. Serve chicken with remaining warmed baste.

Mussels in Beer Broth over Pasta

Makes 4 servings

2 pounds mussels, scrubbed and soaked
8 ounces uncooked fettuccine pasta
2 tablespoons olive oil
1 bottle (12 ounces) beer
⅓ cup chopped onion
1 clove garlic, minced
¼ teaspoon fennel seeds
1 bulb fresh fennel, peeled and cubed
1 cup coarsely chopped fresh plum tomatoes
Chopped fresh parsley and grated
    Parmesan cheese (optional)

1. Discard any mussels that remain open when tapped with fingers. Cook fettuccine according to package directions; drain. Place fettuccine in large bowl; toss with oil. Cover to keep warm.

2. Meanwhile, combine beer, onion, garlic and fennel seeds in large stockpot. Bring to a boil over high heat. Cover; boil 3 minutes. Add mussels. Cover; reduce heat to medium. Cook 5 to 7 minutes or until mussels are opened. Remove mussels from stockpot with slotted spoon; set aside. Discard any unopened mussels.

3. Simmer, uncovered, until liquid is reduced to about 1 cup. Add cubed fennel; simmer 1 to 2 minutes. Add tomatoes; remove from heat.

4. Spoon mussels over noodles; top with sauce. Garnish with parsley and cheese. Serve immediately.

SEAFOOD

Fish & Chips

Makes 4 servings

¾ cup all-purpose flour
½ cup flat beer
  Vegetable oil
4 medium russet potatoes, each cut into
    8 wedges
  Salt
1 egg, separated
1 pound cod fillets, cut into 8 pieces

1. Combine flour, beer and 2 teaspoons oil in small bowl. Cover; refrigerate 1 to 2 hours.

2. Pour 2 inches oil into heavy skillet. Heat over medium heat until fresh bread cube placed in oil browns in 45 seconds (about 365°F). Add enough potato wedges to fit. Do not crowd. Fry potato wedges 4 to 6 minutes or until outsides are brown, turning once. Drain on paper towels; sprinkle lightly with salt. Repeat with remaining potato wedges.* Reserve oil to fry cod.

3. Stir egg yolk into reserved flour mixture. Beat egg white in medium bowl with electric mixer at medium-high speed until soft peaks form. Fold egg white into flour mixture; set aside. Rinse fish; pat dry with paper towels. Dip 4 fish pieces into batter; fry 4 to 6 minutes or until batter is crispy and brown and fish flakes easily with fork, turning once. Drain on paper towels. Repeat with remaining fish pieces.* Serve immediately with potato wedges.

Allow temperature of oil to return to 365°F between batches.

SEAFOOD

Spicy Ale Shrimp

Makes 15 to 20 shrimp

3 bottles (12 ounces each) pilsner beer,
    divided
1 tablespoon seafood boil seasoning blend
1 teaspoon mustard seeds
1 teaspoon red pepper flakes
1 lemon, sliced into quarters
1 pound raw large shrimp (15 to 20 count),
    deveined and shelled except for tails
  Dipping Sauce (recipe follows)

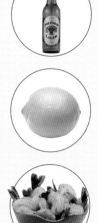

1. Place 2 bottles of beer, seafood boil seasoning, mustard seeds and pepper flakes in large stockpot. Juice lemon into pot; add lemon quarters. Bring beer mixture to boil over medium-high heat.

2. Meanwhile, pour remaining 1 bottle of beer into large bowl half-filled with ice; set aside.

3. Add shrimp to simmering beer mixture; cover and remove from heat. Let sit 3 minutes to cook shrimp. Drain; transfer shrimp to bowl of chilled beer and ice cubes to stop cooking. When cool, remove shrimp from bowl; arrange on platter. Serve with Dipping Sauce.

Dipping Sauce: *Combine 1 cup ketchup, 1 tablespoon chili-garlic paste, 1 tablespoon grated fresh horseradish and juice of 1 lime in small glass bowl. Add hot pepper sauce to taste; mix well. Cover; refrigerate 1 hour. Makes about 1 cup sauce.*

SEAFOOD

Boston Baked Beans

Makes 8 servings

2 cans (about 15 ounces each) navy or Great Northern beans, rinsed and drained
½ cup beer (not dark beer)
⅓ cup minced yellow or red onion
⅓ cup ketchup
3 tablespoons light molasses
2 teaspoons Worcestershire sauce
1 teaspoon dry mustard
½ teaspoon ground ginger
4 slices turkey bacon

1. Preheat oven to 350°F. Place beans in 11×7-inch glass baking dish. Combine beer, onion, ketchup, molasses, Worcestershire sauce, mustard and ginger in medium bowl. Pour over beans; toss to coat.

2. Cut bacon into 1-inch pieces; arrange in single layer over beans. Bake, uncovered, 40 to 45 minutes or until most of liquid is absorbed and bacon is browned.

SIDES

Vegetable-Barley Pilaf

Makes 4 servings

Nonstick cooking spray
¾ cup chopped onion
¾ cup chopped celery
¾ cup sliced mushrooms
1 cup beer
¾ cup sliced yellow summer squash
½ cup quick-cooking barley
½ cup sliced carrots
¼ cup chopped fresh parsley
2 teaspoons chopped fresh basil *or*
    ½ teaspoon dried basil
½ teaspoon chicken bouillon granules
⅛ teaspoon black pepper

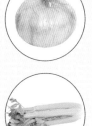

1. Coat large skillet with cooking spray. Add onion, celery and mushrooms; cook and stir over medium heat until vegetables are tender.

2. Stir in beer, squash, barley, carrots, parsley, basil, bouillon granules and pepper. Bring to a boil over high heat. Reduce heat to medium-low. Cover; simmer 10 to 12 minutes or until barley and vegetables are tender.

SIDES

Malty Maple Cornbread

Makes 9 servings

1 cup coarse ground cornmeal
1 cup dark ale or porter
¼ cup maple syrup
1 cup all-purpose flour
½ teaspoon salt
1 tablespoon baking powder
2 large eggs
¼ cup melted butter

1. Preheat oven to 400°F. Grease 9-inch square baking pan. Combine cornmeal, porter and maple syrup in small bowl.

2. Sift flour, salt and baking powder into large bowl. Add cornmeal mixture, eggs and melted butter. Stir until well blended.

3. Pour batter into prepared pan. Bake 20 to 25 minutes or until wooden pick inserted into center comes out clean. Cool 10 minutes. Cut into squares.

Tip: *For an extra-flavorful crust, place the greased pan in the oven for several minutes to preheat. When batter is ready, pour into hot pan and bake as directed. The cornbread will develop a thick, brown crust with a deep, rich flavor.*

German Rye Beer Bread

Makes 12 or 16 servings (1 loaf)

1½-POUND LOAF
- 1¼ cups light beer, at room temperature
- 2 tablespoons light molasses
- 1 tablespoon butter
- 1½ teaspoons salt
- 2 teaspoons caraway seeds
- 2½ cups bread flour
- ½ cup rye flour
- 1½ teaspoons quick-rise active dry yeast

2-POUND LOAF
- 1½ cups light beer, at room temperature
- 3 tablespoons light molasses
- 1½ tablespoons butter
- 2 teaspoons salt
- 1 tablespoon caraway seeds
- 3¼ cups bread flour
- ¾ cup rye flour
- 2 teaspoons quick-rise active dry yeast

BREAD MACHINE DIRECTIONS

1. Measuring carefully, place all ingredients in bread machine pan in order specified by owner's manual.

2. Program basic cycle and desired crust setting; press start. Remove baked bread from pan; cool on wire rack.

SIDES

Pilsner Parmesan Potatoes

Makes 4 to 6 servings

4 pounds Yukon Gold potatoes, peeled and thinly sliced
1 cup minced Vidalia onion
1 cup grated fresh Parmesan cheese
12 ounces pilsner beer
½ cup whipping cream
1 tablespoon all-purpose flour
1 teaspoon paprika
Salt and pepper to taste

1. Preheat oven to 350°F. Butter 13×9-inch baking dish. Place potato slices in prepared dish. Sprinkle with minced onion.

2. Combine Parmesan cheese, beer, cream, flour, paprika, salt and pepper in medium bowl. Pour over potato mixture; stir gently to coat potato slices evenly. Cover baking dish with foil.

3. Bake 30 minutes. Remove foil; bake 15 to 20 minutes more or until potatoes are golden brown and bubbly. Remove from oven; let stand 15 minutes before serving.

SIDES

Cheddar and Leek Strata

Makes 12 servings

8 eggs, lightly beaten
2 cups milk
½ cup beer or ale
2 cloves garlic, minced
¼ teaspoon salt
¼ teaspoon black pepper
1 loaf (16 ounces) sourdough bread, cut into
    ½-inch cubes
2 small leeks, coarsely chopped
1 red bell pepper, chopped
1½ cups (6 ounces) shredded Swiss cheese
1½ cups (6 ounces) shredded sharp Cheddar
    cheese
Fresh sage sprigs (optional)

1. Combine eggs, milk, beer, garlic, salt and black pepper in large bowl. Beat until well blended.

2. Place ½ of bread cubes on bottom of greased 13×9-inch baking dish. Sprinkle ½ of leeks and ½ of bell pepper over bread cubes. Top with ¾ cup Swiss cheese and ¾ cup Cheddar cheese. Repeat layers with remaining ingredients, ending with Cheddar cheese. Pour egg mixture evenly over top. Cover tightly with plastic wrap or foil. Weigh top of strata down with slightly smaller baking dish. Refrigerate strata at least 2 hours or overnight.

3. Preheat oven to 350°F. Bake, uncovered, 40 to 45 minutes or until center is set. Garnish with sage. Serve immediately.

SIDES

Asparagus with Honey-Garlic Sauce

Makes 4 servings

1 pound asparagus
¼ cup Dijon mustard
¼ cup dark ale or beer
3 tablespoons honey
½ teaspoon minced garlic
¼ teaspoon crushed dried thyme leaves
¼ teaspoon salt

Add asparagus to boiling, salted water and cook, covered, about 2 minutes or until barely tender. Drain. Combine mustard, ale, honey, garlic, thyme and salt; mix well. Pour over cooked asparagus.

Favorite recipe from **National Honey Board**

Wisconsin Sausage Soup

Makes 8 to 10 servings

½ cup butter
1 onion, chopped
1 carrot, chopped
1 teaspoon minced garlic
1 cup all-purpose flour
2 cups chicken broth
2 cups milk
¾ cup beer
1 teaspoon Worcestershire sauce
½ teaspoon salt
½ teaspoon dry mustard
1 bay leaf
7 ounces Cheddar cheese, shredded
3 ounces Swiss cheese, shredded
½ pound **HILLSHIRE FARM**® Smoked Sausage

Melt butter in medium saucepan over medium heat. Add onion, carrot and garlic; sauté until softened. Add flour; cook 5 minutes, stirring often. Add chicken broth, milk, beer, Worcestershire sauce, salt, mustard and bay leaf. Reduce heat to low; cook until soup has thickened, whisking often. Remove and discard bay leaves.

Slowly whisk cheeses into soup until combined and smooth. Cut Smoked Sausage lengthwise into quarters, then slice into ½-inch pieces. Sauté sausage in small skillet over medium-high heat until heated through. Blot excess grease with paper towels; add sausage to soup. Serve soup hot.

SOUPS

Beer and Cheese Soup

Makes 6 (1-cup) servings

2 to 3 slices pumpernickel or rye bread
3 tablespoons water
3 tablespoons cornstarch
¼ cup finely chopped onion
1 tablespoon butter or margarine
¾ teaspoon dried thyme leaves
2 cloves garlic, minced
1 can (about 14 ounces each) chicken broth
1 cup beer
6 ounces American cheese, shredded or diced
4 to 6 ounces sharp Cheddar cheese, shredded
½ teaspoon paprika
1 cup milk

1. Preheat oven to 425°F. Slice bread into ½-inch cubes; place on baking sheet. Bake 10 to 12 minutes, or until crisp, stirring once; set aside.

2. While bread is in oven, stir water into cornstarch in small bowl; set aside. Place onion, butter, thyme and garlic in 3-quart saucepan; cook over medium-high heat 3 to 4 minutes or until onion is tender. Add broth; bring to a boil. Stir in beer, cheeses and paprika. Reduce heat to low; whisk in milk and cornstarch mixture. Stir until cheese melts and soup bubbles and thickens. Ladle into bowls. Top with croutons.

SOUPS

Hearty Beefy Beer Soup

Makes 6 servings

1 tablespoon vegetable oil
¾ pound round steak, cut into ½-inch cubes
1 large onion, chopped
2 medium carrots, sliced
2 ribs celery, diced
5 cups beef broth
1 can (12 ounces) beer
¾ teaspoon dried oregano leaves
¼ teaspoon salt
⅛ teaspoon black pepper
1 small zucchini, cut into ½-inch cubes
4 ounces mushrooms, sliced
1 can (15 ounces) kidney beans, rinsed and
   drained
   Fresh herb sprig (optional)

1. Heat oil in 5-quart Dutch oven over medium heat. Add beef, onion, carrots and celery to hot oil. Cook and stir until meat is no longer pink and carrots and celery are slightly tender. Remove from heat.

2. Stir in beef broth, beer, oregano, salt and pepper. Bring to a boil over high heat. Reduce heat to medium-low; simmer, uncovered, 45 minutes.

3. Stir zucchini, mushrooms and kidney beans into soup. Bring to a boil over high heat. Reduce heat to medium-low; simmer, uncovered, about 5 minutes or until zucchini is tender. Ladle into bowls. Garnish with herb sprig.

SOUPS

Ham and Beer Cheese Soup

Makes 8 servings

1 cup chopped onion
½ cup sliced celery
2 tablespoons butter or margarine
1 cup hot water
1 HERB-OX® chicken flavor bouillon cube or
    1 teaspoon instant chicken bouillon
3 cups half-and-half
3 cups (18 ounces) diced CURE 81® ham
1 (16-ounce) loaf pasteurized process cheese
    spread, cubed
1 (12-ounce) can beer
3 tablespoons all-purpose flour
    Popcorn (optional)

In Dutch oven over medium-high heat, sauté onion
and celery in butter until tender. In small liquid
measuring cup, combine water and bouillon; set
aside. Add half-and-half, ham, cheese, beer and
¾ cup broth to onion and celery mixture. Cook,
stirring constantly, until cheese melts. Combine
remaining ¼ cup broth and flour; stir until smooth.
Add flour mixture to soup, stirring constantly.
Cook, stirring constantly, until slightly thickened.
Sprinkle individual servings with popcorn, if
desired.

SOUPS